ITALY

ITALY

THE BIRTHPLACE
OF THE RENAISSANCE

CLAUDIA MARTIN

amber
BOOKS

Published by
Amber Books Ltd
United House
North Road
London
N7 9DP
United Kingdom
www.amberbooks.co.uk
Instagram: amberbooksltd
Facebook: amberbooks
Twitter: @amberbooks

Project Editor: Sarah Uttridge
Designer: Jerry Williams
Picture Research: Terry Forshaw, Justin Willsdon

ISBN: 978-1-78274-663-8

Printed in China

4 6 8 10 9 7 5

Contents

Introduction

Some might say there have been two momentous periods when Italy led – and irrevocably changed – the world. The first of these periods would be the days, from around 100 BC to AD 400, when Rome was the largest city in the world. Roman customs, language, law, engineering and architecture were marched across the vast Roman lands in Europe, North Africa and Western Asia. The second period was the Renaissance, an age of 'rebirth' which took root in Florence and other Italian cities in the 14th century. The peninsula's painters, sculptors, architects, poets, educators, diplomats and scientists returned to the learning of the classical Romans and Greeks, building on it with their own extraordinary humanism, creativity and reasoning.

Yet, Italy has never ceased to excel and to challenge all expectations of what is possible, from the powerhouse Etruscan cities of the 8th century BC to the soaring tower houses of medieval San Gimignano; from the perfect Baroque townscapes of Sicily's Val di Noto to today's sinuous skyscrapers and endlessly inventive art, film, fashion and cuisine.

ABOVE:
San Gimignano, Tuscany.
RIGHT:
Rome, the capital city of Italy.

Central Italy: Heart of the Nation

At the heart of Italy both geographically and culturally is Rome, once the centre of an empire that left an indelible mark on Italy, Europe and the world. Evidence of the ingenuity of ancient engineers includes the virtuoso dome of the Pantheon and the arcaded Colosseum. Every age added something more to Rome's treasure trove, from the Renaissance's exuberant Sistine Chapel to the Baroque Trevi Fountain.

North of Rome are the regions of Tuscany and Umbria, where vineyards and olive groves give way to more rugged Apennine landscapes in the east. From the earliest times, the people of central Italy retreated into hilltop settlements for defence. Today, perfectly preserved hilltowns such as San Gimignano, Volterra and Orvieto still mark the skyline.

In the Middle Ages, the Tuscan city of Pisa celebrated its Golden Age, resulting in the magnificent wedding-cake façades of its Campo dei Miracoli ('Field of Miracles'). As Pisa's importance waned, Florence's grew. It became the birthplace of the Renaissance style of architecture, where the architect Filippo Brunelleschi created the radical dome of the cathedral of Santa Maria del Fiore, drawing on the Pantheon for inspiration.

OPPOSITE:
Pienza, Tuscany
In 1459, Pope Pius II embarked on the complete remodelling of the village of his birthplace, turning it into a Renaissance 'new town' and renaming it Pienza, after himself. Pius employed the architect Bernardo Rossellino to create palaces, a cathedral and a town hall, set around a trapezoidal piazza. The result was a masterpiece of urban planning.

Roman Forum, Rome, Lazio
For centuries, the Forum was the centre of ancient Rome. Today, the ruins of government, commercial and religious buildings still cluster around the central square, once the site of the market as well as a meeting place for politics, business or unrest. In the foreground are the eight remaining columns of the front porch of the Temple of Saturn.

OPPOSITE:

Pantheon, Rome

Finished in around 125 AD, the Pantheon is one of the most complete ancient Roman structures, thanks in part to its continuous use, first as a temple and today as a church. The extraordinary dome, which opens to the sky through its *oculus*, is the world's largest unreinforced concrete dome.

RIGHT:

St Peter's Basilica, Vatican City

Built on the believed burial site of St Peter, the basilica was designed by the greatest 16th- and 17th-century architects, notably Donato Bramante, Michelangelo, Gian Lorenzo Bernini and Carlo Maderno. The dome, inspired by those of the Pantheon and of Florence's Duomo, is the tallest in the world, at 136.6m (448ft) high.

LEFT:

Centro storico, Rome
In the knotted medieval backstreets and blind alleys of the *centro storico*, pedestrians must be constantly on the lookout for speeding mopeds. With their crisscrossing arches, the ochre-, rose- and gold-plastered homes seem to press up against each other for support.

BELOW:

Pons Fabricius, Rome
Rome's oldest bridge, the Pons Fabricius was built in 62 BC and has been in continuous use. It spans half the width of the River Tiber, from the Campus Martius to Tiber Island. The small arch in the central pier was designed to let high water flow through, reducing pressure on the bridge itself.

OPPOSITE:

Trevi Fountain, Rome
In 1730, Pope Clement XII launched a competition to design a new fountain at the junction of three roads (*tre vie*). Baroque architect Nicola Salvi was awarded the commission. The theme of the fountain is the taming of the waters, with a giant figure of Oceanus at its centre.

Ponte Sisto, Rome

The Renaissance Ponte Sisto connects the *centro storico* with Trastevere, on the west bank of the Tiber. In ancient times, this was a multicultural, artisan area, outside the city walls. Today, the neighbourhood is known for its nightlife. In the background is the floodlit dome of St Peter's in Vatican City, also on the west bank of the Tiber and established as a sovereign state in 1929.

Spanish Steps, Rome

Named in honour of the Spanish Embassy at their base, the Baroque Spanish Steps descend from the church of Trinità dei Monti to the Piazza di Spagna. The steps were designed to make the drop from the church to the streets below appear less severe, a problem solved by the clever use of terraces and gently undulating widths.

**Palazzo dell'INA,
EUR, Rome**
The EUR (Exposizione
Universale Roma) business
district, to the south of central
Rome, was conceived as the
site of the 1942 world fair,
which was to be opened by
Benito Mussolini. World
War II put a stop to both
the fair and the building
work. During the 1950s and
60s, the unfinished Fascist
buildings were completed,
creating a unique cityscape of
Rationalist urban planning.

Palazzo della Civiltà Italiana, EUR

The monumental Fascist design of the 'Palace of Italian Civilization' was conceived in 1937 by architects Giovanni Guerrini, Ernesto Lapadula and Mario Romano. After completion, the building stood empty for a decade, but is today the headquarters of luxury fashion house Fendi.

Palazzo dei Congressi, EUR

Although construction started on this *palazzo* in 1938, it was not completed until 1954. The building encloses a vast open space of 2000sq m (21,500sq ft), making it a favoured location for sports events, conferences and fashion shows.

LEFT:

Christian basilica, Ostia Antica

Ostia Antica was the port of ancient Rome, lying at the mouth of the Tiber. Now the extensive archaeological site is 3km (2 miles) inland, due to the silting of the river. This three-naved basilica dates from around 350 AD.

LEFT BELOW:

House of Diana, Ostia Antica

The House of Diana (on the right side of the street) is named after the terracotta relief of the goddess Diana in one of its courtyards. Archaeologists believe the building was a three-storeyed apartment block, or *insula*, with shops on its ground floor and dwelling places for ordinary citizens above.

RIGHT:

Street, Ostia Antica

In ancient times, Ostia was home to grain, wine and oil merchants, ship-fitters and rope-makers, as well as the officials, slaves, actors and bath-house keepers needed to service a bustling city of some 50,000 inhabitants.

LEFT:

Hadrian's Villa, Tivoli, Lazio
Around 30km (18 miles) from ancient Rome, Tivoli was a popular retirement spot for wealthy Romans. In the 2nd century AD, Emperor Hadrian often retreated here to a sumptuous villa and landscaped estate that he had helped to design. This is the so-called 'Maritime Theatre', a circular enclosure containing a library, lounge, art gallery, heated baths and splendid fountain.

OPPOSITE:

Villa d'Este, Tivoli, Lazio
Tivoli remained a popular summer retreat for many centuries. In the 16th century, Cardinal Ippolito d'Este commissioned a Renaissance villa and gardens that almost eclipsed Hadrian's Villa in their scope and beauty. Here the three fishponds can be seen behind the 20th-century Fountain of Neptune.

Perugia, Umbria
The capital of Umbria, Perugia was a key city for the Etruscans, who held sway over western Umbria, Tuscany and northern Lazio from around 800 BC until Rome gradually wrested control. The Etruscans built walls so sturdy around Perugia that large sections have survived to this day. This panorama of the city was taken from the Porta Sole gate.

LEFT:

Medieval arch, Perugia
In the Middle Ages, Perugia became an important independent city, with its university established in 1308. The city was often embroiled in petty fights with other Umbrian towns, as well as being riven by feuds between its own rival families, the Oddi and Baglioni.

RIGHT:

Aqueduct, Via Appia, Perugia
In the 13th century, the officials of Perugia decided to build an aqueduct to bring fresh water from a mountain spring 8km (5 miles) away into the centre of the city. The structure terminated at the monumental Fontana Maggiore in the city's main square. One of the sturdy arches of the aqueduct straddles Via Appia.

Upper Church, Basilica of St Francis, Assisi, Umbria

The Basilica of St Francis was started in 1228, two years after the death of St Francis, founder of the Franciscan order. The saint is buried in the crypt of the Lower Church, while the Upper Church is adorned with a fresco cycle of the life of the saint, mostly attributed to Giotto. To the right of this photograph can be seen his *Vision of the Flaming Chariot*.

Basilica of St Francis and Piazza Inferiore, Assisi

The arcades of the 'Lower Square' were built in 1474 to house stalls that furnished the needs of the many pilgrims to the basilica. The Lower Church, which was built first, is entered through the Gothic doorway, surrounded by a later Renaissance porch, at the end of the Lower Square. Directly above the Lower Church is the pale form of the Romanesque Upper Church.

LEFT:

Basilica of St Clare, Assisi
The remains of St Clare of Assisi are kept in a shrine in the crypt of the basilica that bears her name. St Clare was a follower of St Francis who founded the Order of Poor Ladies, commonly known as the Order of Poor Clares, when she was just 17.

OPPOSITE:

Abbey of St Peter, Assisi
After the end of the 13th century, any order that was not Franciscan was forbidden from building in Assisi. Luckily, the Benedictine Order had already consecrated their Romanesque-Gothic Abbey of St Peter in 1253. It can be seen at the left of this panorama.

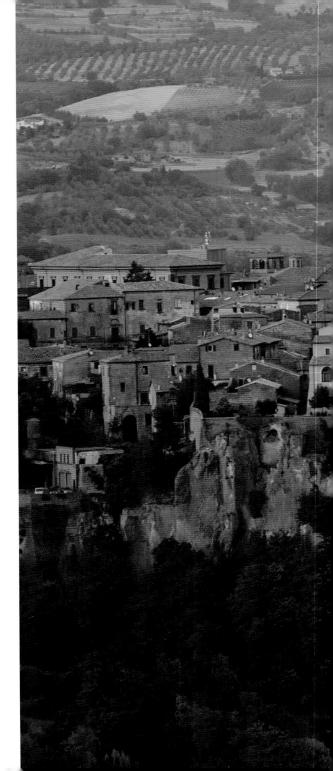

LEFT:

Cathedral of Orvieto, Umbria

The *duomo* of Orvieto was constructed in the 14th century on the orders of Pope Urban IV. Its façade is a glorious Gothic concoction of intricately carved polychrome stone, columns, gables, mosaics, bas-reliefs and sculptures. This winged bronze ox by Lorenzo Maitani represents St Luke.

LEFT BELOW:

The Last Judgement, Orvieto Cathedral

This bas-relief of sinners at the Last Judgement, on the fourth pier of the cathedral's façade, is the work of unknown masters and their workshops. The sinners are being taken to hell by horrible devils, a scene designed to fill worshippers with fear.

RIGHT:

Orvieto

The old town of Orvieto sits on top of a butte of volcanic rock that rises 300m (980ft) from the surrounding valley. Much of the town is built from the same dark volcanic tuff. The multicoloured façade of the cathedral, with its shimmering mosaics, dwarfs the surrounding buildings.

Viareggio, Tuscany
Viareggio first saw popularity
as a resort in the 19th century,
although much of its grand
seafront boulevard was built
in the early 20th century
in elegant Art Nouveau
style. In high summer, it
can cost as much as £20 to
rent an obligatory parasol
and lounger for a day on
Viareggio's wide beach.

**Viareggio and
the Apuan Alps**
The resort is backed by the
Apuan Alps, a 55km-long
(34-mile) chain that stretches
through northern Tuscany.
Around 25 million years ago,
intense pressure transformed
much of the mountains'
limestone into marble. The
stone is quarried in the area
of Carrara, from where stone
was taken for use in Rome's
Pantheon, Michelangelo's
David and Siena's cathedral.

Vineyard, Tuscany
Although mountainous in parts, Tuscany's landscape is dominated by rolling hills with soils rich in minerals. Cereals, potatoes, olives and grapes are key crops. Well-known Tuscan wines include Chianti, Vino Nobile di Montepulciano and Brunello di Montalcino, which are all made largely with the Sangiovese grape.

OPPOSITE:
Orcia Valley, Tuscany
The Orcia Valley is a UNESCO World Heritage Site due to the fact that its landscapes were depicted time and again by Renaissance painters, influencing the very way that we view humanity's relationship with nature. Cypress trees have come to be a symbol of this valley.

Siena, Tuscany

By the 13th century, Siena was one of the largest and most powerful cities in Europe; it controlled the regional wool industry and was a major centre for banking. In the late 13th and early 14th centuries, the city embarked on a dramatic overhaul, constructing its ambitious cathedral and its huge central piazza, called the Campo, which is the site of the twice-yearly bareback horse race known as the Palio.

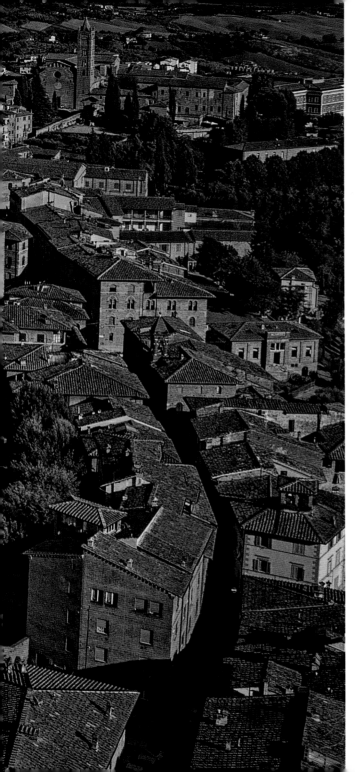

LEFT:

Rooftops, Siena
During medieval times, Siena was divided into 17 *contrade*, or districts, with each one responsible for aspects of the city's defence. The tradition of *contrade* is still strong today, particularly during the Palio horse race, when 10 districts are drawn by lot to take part.

RIGHT ABOVE:

Torre del Mangia, Siena
The Torre del Mangia is glimpsed from the courtyard of the Palazzo Pubblico, the focal point of Siena's Piazza del Campo. The tower's name translates as 'Tower of the Eater', after its first bellringer, Giovanni di Balduccio, who was known for his hearty appetite and extravagance.

RIGHT BELOW:

Cathedral, Siena
The richly decorated façade of the 13th-century cathedral was designed by Giovanni Pisano, whose workshop carved the countless statues of prophets, philosophers and apostles. The marble is laid in stripes of white, greenish-black and red. The three large mosaics on the gables were added in the 19th century.

**Ponte Vecchio,
Florence, Tuscany**
The 'Old Bridge' across the
River Arno was built in 1345
to replace an earlier, damaged
structure. The arched bridge
was overloaded with shops
from its earliest days. These
were butchers, fishmongers
and tanners until 1593,
when these malodorous
enterprises were banned in
favour of goldsmiths.

LEFT:

Baptistery door, Florence
The Florentine sculptor and goldsmith Lorenzo Ghiberti is best known for the two pairs of bronze doors that he created for Florence's baptistery. The east doors, for which he used the recently discovered principles of perspective, are decorated with panels containing scenes from the Old Testament and were completed in 1452. This detail depicts Moses receiving the Ten Commandments.

LEFT BELOW:

Backstreet, Florence
Tuscan cooking places its emphasis on using high-quality, fresh local ingredients, including *zolfino* beans, red potatoes and *costoluto* tomatoes. These, alongside stale bread, can be mixed into *ribollita* soup, once a traditional 'peasant' food but today served in fine Florentine restaurants.

RIGHT:

Skyline, Florence
The Duomo, also known as Santa Maria del Fiore, seems to hover over the ruddy roofs of the city. Just a stroll away down Via dei Calzaiuoli is the Palazzo Vecchio, the city's castle-like town hall with its 94-m (308-ft) tower. A replica of Michelangelo's *David* stands in front of the building in the Piazza della Signoria, while the original remains safe in the Accademia gallery to the north of the Duomo.

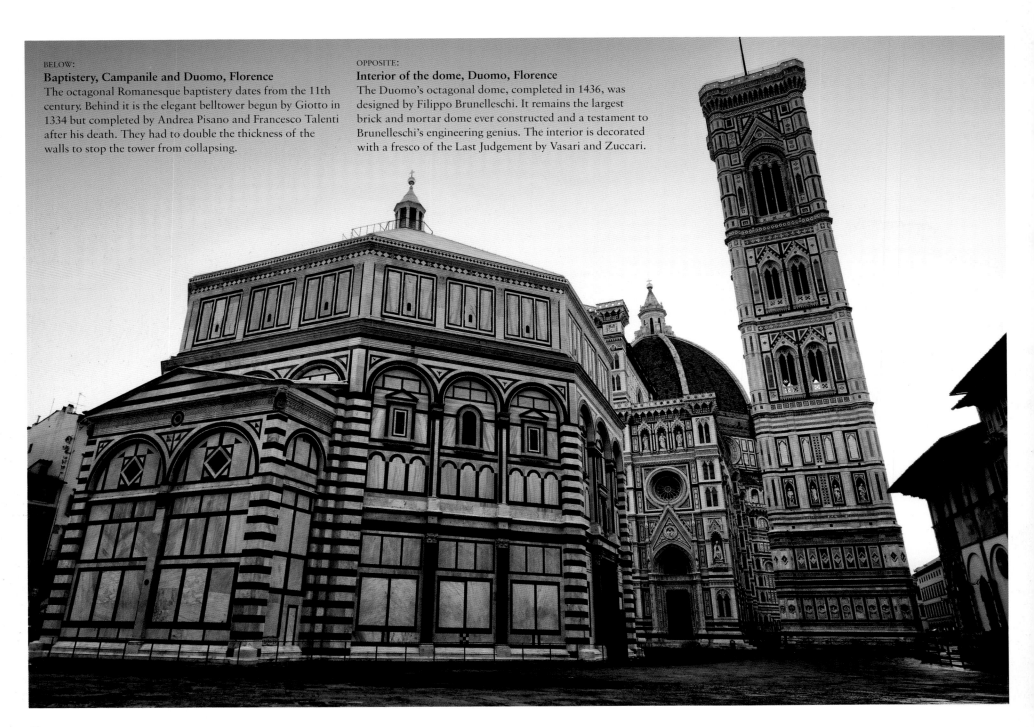

BELOW:

Baptistery, Campanile and Duomo, Florence
The octagonal Romanesque baptistery dates from the 11th century. Behind it is the elegant belltower begun by Giotto in 1334 but completed by Andrea Pisano and Francesco Talenti after his death. They had to double the thickness of the walls to stop the tower from collapsing.

OPPOSITE:

Interior of the dome, Duomo, Florence
The Duomo's octagonal dome, completed in 1436, was designed by Filippo Brunelleschi. It remains the largest brick and mortar dome ever constructed and a testament to Brunelleschi's engineering genius. The interior is decorated with a fresco of the Last Judgement by Vasari and Zuccari.

Cathedral and Leaning Tower, Pisa, Tuscany

Begun in 1173, the Leaning Tower started to subside when only three of its eight storeys had been constructed, but it leant in the opposite direction from today. Slanted stones were inserted to correct the problem, which resulted in the tower keeling the opposite way. By 1990, the tower was a dangerous 4.5m (15ft) from vertical. A massive and costly rescue operation took place, involving steel supports, lead counterweights and the removal of water and silt from the foundations.

San Miniato, Tuscany

In medieval times, the village of San Miniato was of great strategic importance, perched on three hilltops, halfway between Pisa and Florence and at the confluence of the Rivers Arno and Elsa. The restored red-brick belltower of the cathedral offers unmissable views over the valley.

LEFT:

Ponte della Maddalena, Borgo a Mozzano, Tuscany
This bridge is known locally as the Ponte del Diavolo ('Devil's Bridge'). According to legend, its builders found the work so difficult they asked the devil for help. In return, the devil asked for the soul of the first living being to cross the bridge. To cheat the devil of his human soul, bread was thrown onto the completed bridge to lure a dog. In reality, the bridge was built in the late 11th century as a crossing over the River Serchio for those travelling the Via Francigena pilgrimage route from France to Rome.

RIGHT:

San Gimignano, Tuscany
The walled hilltown of San Gimignano is known as the 'Town of Fine Towers' due to the unique preservation of its medieval tower houses. Such dwellings were built in other medieval towns by wealthy families as a symbol of their power, but most collapsed or were torn down – in San Gimignano, 14 survive. During the town's heyday, there were 72. The tallest is the 54-m (177-ft) Torre Grossa, completed in 1300.

LEFT:

Palazzo Pretorio, Volterra, Tuscany
On the central square of the Etruscan town of Volterra is the Palazzo Pretorio, with its Torre del Porcellino ('Piglet's Tower'). The tower got its name from the carved boar standing on a little shelf near its summit.

OPPOSITE:

Val di Cecina near Volterra
The valley of the River Cecina is characterized by volcanic hills, punctuated by steep ravines and cliffs. The world's first geothermal energy power plant was built nearby, in a region known as the Valle del Diavolo ('Devil's Valley'), in 1911.

LEFT:

Gran Sasso d'Italia, Abruzzo
This barren mountain's name translates as 'Great Rock of Italy'. With an elevation of 2912m (9554ft), it is the highest peak in continental Italy south of the Alps. The surrounding area and its wildlife – including the Abruzzo chamois and critically endangered Marsican bear – are protected by national park status.

BELOW:

Calascio, Abruzzo
The once-abandoned village of Calascio is most famous for its fortress, the Rocca Calascio, which dates from the 13th century. It is the highest fortress in the Apennines, constructed to watch over the Navelli plain. Seemingly impregnable, it was partially destroyed during an immense earthquake in 1461. The site has been used as a location in several films, including 1986's *The Name of the Rose*.

OPPOSITE:

Monti Sibillini, Le Marche
Dotted with dramatically sited hill villages, such as Arquata del Tronto and Montemonaco, the Monti Sibillini national park is one of Italy's most beautiful. The scenery is dominated by glacier-worn U-shaped valleys, where hikers and rafters enjoy spectacular caves and gorges.

Central Apennines

The backbone of Italy, the Apennine range runs for 1200km (750 miles) down the length of the peninsula. The mountains have preserved some of the most intact montane forests and grasslands in the whole of Europe. Here are 1800 plant species, including lizard and tongue orchids, as well as some of the last refuges for the vulnerable Italian wolf and other large carnivores.

Northwest Italy: Wealth and Beauty

This region is home to Italy's two wealthiest cities, Milan and Turin. These are hard-working, style-conscious towns with more than their fair share of elegant shopping streets, world-class museums and genteel cafés. To the north of Milan are two of Italy's most exquisite and most visited lakes, Como and Maggiore. To the south is the port of Genoa, rougher around the edges, where faded merchants' *palazzi* rub shoulders with dusty workshops and performance spaces.

Genoa is the capital of Liguria, a crescent-shaped region that hogs the northwestern coast. Here is the Italian Riviera, stretching from glamorous San Remo to the Cinque Terre ('Five Lands'), named for the five villages that teeter breathtakingly on the steep cliffs.

Inland, the River Po flows eastward across a wide plain, finally reaching the Adriatic Sea south of Venice. The source of the Po is in the Alps, which stretch in a great arc across northern Italy, straddling the borders with France, Switzerland, Austria and Slovenia. Monte Bianco ('Mont Blanc' to the French), Western Europe's highest peak at 4808m (15,774ft), is shared between France and Italy. Nearby, Italy's oldest national park, the Parco Nazionale del Gran Paradiso, was established in 1922 to protect the Alpine ibex.

OPPOSITE:
Sacra di San Michele, Piemonte
The fortified Abbey of St Michael, built from the 10th to the 15th centuries, can be reached by 243 steps carved into the rock, chillingly named the Scalone dei Morti ('Stairs of the Dead'). The bodies of deceased monks were laid here so that local people could be reminded of their own mortality.

**Milan and the
Po Valley, Lombardy**
Lombardy is the richest and
most populous of Italy's
20 regions. The country's
longest river, the Po, provides
irrigation for the valley's green
farmland and hydroelectric
power for its many factories,
such as Alfa Romeo and Pirelli
near Milan.

LEFT:

Porta Nuova, Milan
In 2005, Milan embarked on a major redevelopment of abandoned railyards to the north of the city centre and close to the main train station. The result was the Porta Nuova Garibaldi district, home to sleek skyscrapers by architect César Pelli.

OPPOSITE:

Naviglio Grande, Milan
Construction began on the Naviglio Grande canal in 1177. It stretches 50km (30 miles) from the River Ticino to Milan's Ticinese dock. Today, Milan's Navigli neighbourhood is filled with cafés, galleries, antique shops and markets.

LEFT:

Via Dante, Milan

Milan is the world's fashion capital, boasting the internationally renowned Milan Fashion Weeks and the headquarters of houses such as Armani, Prada, Valentino and Versace. The fashion industry boomed here in the 1950s, as Milan, already Italy's most industrial city, also became its most dynamic.

ABOVE:

Cheese market, Milan

Lombardy is one of Italy's most important cheese-making regions. Internationally known cheeses from the region include Gorgonzola, Grana Padano, Taleggio and Mascarpone. The last is a cream cheese used to thicken risotto as well as in desserts such as tiramisu and semifreddo.

OPPOSITE:

Galleria Vittorio Emanuele II, Milan

This 1877 shopping mall was conceived as a covered walkway to link the cathedral with La Scala opera house. It was designed by Giuseppe Mengoni, who unfortunately fell to his death from the roof. The mall is named after the first king of the newly united Kingdom of Italy, formed in 1861.

Milan Cathedral

Taking six centuries to complete, the *duomo* is the largest cathedral in Italy (the larger St Peter's is in Vatican City). The five aisles are divided by 52 immense piers. Due to the length of time that work continued on the cathedral, it is in a hotchpotch of styles, from the Baroque–Gothic decoration of its façade to its masterful Renaissance 'Amadeo's' spire.

Santa Maria delle Grazie, Milan

Known as the Chiostro delle Rane ('Cloister of Frogs'), the tranquil 15th-century cloisters of Santa Maria delle Grazie were designed by Donato Bramante. The convent is best known for being the location of Leonardo da Vinci's dramatic *Last Supper* (1490s). In the mural, the face of Judas was apparently modelled on the convent's prior.

OPPOSITE:

Palazzo Lombardia, Milan
Completed in 2011, the headquarters of the regional government was designed by Pei Cobb Freed & Partners. The sinuously curving forms of lightweight plastic and metal are intended to evoke the rivers and landscapes of Lombardy. This central plaza also echoes Milan's groundbreaking Galleria Vittorio Emanuele II.

BELOW:

San Siro Stadium, Milan
The home of AC and Inter Milan, this stadium has a seating capacity of 80,000, making it Italy's largest. Construction began in 1925, but the current roof, with its distinctive jutting red girders, was added in time for the 1990 World Cup. The stadium has hosted four European Cup Finals, in 1965, 1970, 2001 and 2016.

RIGHT:

Bosco Verticale, Porta Nuova, Milan
The award-winning 'Vertical Forest' is a pair of skyscrapers in the redeveloped Porta Nuova district. The residential towers, which opened in 2014, are planted with 900 trees on their steel-reinforced concrete balconies. The trees mitigate pollution and moderate noise and temperature in the costly apartments.

Lake Como, Lombardy
Although it is 46km (29 miles) long, Como is the smallest of the 'big three' Italian lakes – the other two being Maggiore and Garda. The lake has been a popular retreat for the wealthy since Roman times, when author and magistrate Pliny the Younger built two villas by the lake, called 'Comedy' and 'Tragedy'.

LEFT:

Moltrasio, Lake Como
On the western shore of the lake, not far from the border with Switzerland, is the town of Moltrasio. Nearby are the Villa Passalacqua, home to opera composer Vincenzo Bellini; Villa Le Rose, which hosted Winston Churchill; and Villa Fontanella, once home to the fashion designer Gianni Versace.

RIGHT ABOVE:

Gardens of Villa del Balbianello, Lake Como
The romantic terraced gardens of the Villa del Balbianello have been used as a location in films such as *Casino Royale* (2006) and *Star Wars: Episode II Attack of the Clones* (2002). To enjoy the full effect, many visitors to the villa arrive by water taxi.

RIGHT BELOW:

Santa Maria del Tiglio, Gravedona, Lake Como
This Romanesque church was built in the 12th century. Unusually, the belltower has a square base but an octagonal upper storey, probably added at a later date.

LEFT:

Belltower, Lake Como
Today, the one-time fishing villages that dot the shores of Como are popular with tourists and windsurfers, who take advantage of the lake's strong winds. The locals give their winds names, including *tivano*, the morning breeze, and *breva*, the ever-changing afternoon wind.

OPPOSITE:

Lake Como and the Alps
In the foothills of the snow-capped Alps, Como is shaped like an upside-down Y. The closest glacier to the lake is on Pizzo Ferrè, a short drive to the north and only a few metres from the Swiss border.

OPPOSITE:

Varenna, Lake Como

The fishermen's houses of Varenna are painted in eye-catching bright colours, as well as the more usual ochre. The town's quiet pedestrian streets climb steeply as they head towards the church from the *gelaterie* and cafés on the lakeshore.

RIGHT:

Bellagio, Lake Como

Positioned on the tip of the triangular piece of land that divides the Como and Lecco branches of the lake, Bellagio is often named as the most beautiful town in Italy. Despite its souvenir shops, Bellagio's stepped, cobbled streets are still charming, particularly after the daytrippers have left for the night.

**Chianale,
Valle Varaita, Piemonte**
Nearly on the border with France, Chianale is the highest village in the Varaita Valley, with an elevation of 1614m (5295ft). Close by is the Alevè Forest, the largest Swiss stone pine forest in the Alps. The oldest pine in the Alevè is believed to be more than 600 years old.

**Gran Paradiso
National Park,
Piemonte and Valle d'Aosta**
Italy's first national park spreads across three valleys at the foot of the Monte Gran Paradiso. Its ecosystems include beech forest, coniferous forest dominated by Norway spruce and Swiss pine, alpine meadow and, higher still, glaciers.

**Male Alpine ibex,
Gran Paradiso**
The Gran Paradiso park owes its existence to King Vittorio Emanuele III, who donated a royal hunting reserve to the state in order to protect the dwindling population of Alpine ibex from poachers. There are now almost 4000 of these intrepid mountain goats in the park.

Turin, Piemonte
Soaring over Turin's cityscape is the domed and spired Mole Antonelliana, which now houses the National Cinema Museum, making this monumental building (*mole*) the tallest museum in the world. In the foreground is the immense Piazza Vittorio Veneto, while the Alps form a dramatic backdrop.

OPPOSITE:

Piazza San Carlo, Turin
On either side of an equestrian statue of the Savoy duke Emanuele Filiberto are the twin Baroque churches of Santa Cristina (left) and San Carlo Borromeo. The slightly more elaborate 18th-century façade of Santa Cristina is decorated with statues of saints and virtues.

BELOW:

Gran Madre di Dio, Turin
The stolid 19th-century Neoclassical church of Gran Madre faces the Ponte Vittorio Emanuele I across the River Po. During the French occupation of Turin from 1802 to 1814, Napoleon himself ordered the building of the bridge, which was completed in 1813.

RIGHT:

Piazza Carlo Emanuele II, Turin
The Savoy dukes initiated a great expansion of the city in 1673. This square was envisaged as the main public space of the 'new' city. The central statue commemorates the liberal 19th-century politician Camillo Benso di Cavour.

BELOW:
Regio Theatre, Turin

The current Regio Theatre was designed in 1967 by architect Carlo Mollino after the previous building was destroyed by fire. The interior sports a space-age acoustic shell to improve the sound quality for its world-renowned operatic performances.

OPPOSITE:
Galleria San Federico, Turin

Built in the 1930s, the Art Deco *galleria* houses shops, offices and the historic 1934 Cinema Lux. The glass roof is an elliptical barrel vault, with domes at the three entrances as well as a large central dome to flood the interior with light.

Cannobio, Lake Maggiore, Piemonte
The lakefront promenade of Cannobio is lined with 18th- and 19th-century houses painted in pastel shades. At the right-hand side is the Santuario della Pietà, which was built to house a painting depicting the Pietà (the Virgin Mary holding the body of Jesus) that was seen to bleed in 1522.

LEFT:

Santa Caterina del Sasso, Lake Maggiore, Lombardy
This convent was carved from the rock face in the 14th century. It is reached by elevator, by a winding stairway or by the boats that dock at its pier. The entrance to the complex is through a portico with four elegant Renaissance arches.

OPPOSITE:

Maccagno, Lake Maggiore, Lombardy
On the eastern shore of the lake is Maccagno, with a peaceful promenade giving unmissable views of the water and mountains. Quieter than other lake towns, Maccagno is a hub for hikers and climbers, who head into the unspoilt hills and valleys in the hinterland.

LEFT:
Isola Bella, Lake Maggiore, Piemonte
In a bay on the western lake, Isola Bella was transformed in the 17th century, when the Borromeo family created fantasy Baroque gardens and a luxurious *palazzo* on the island. The gardens boast the Teatro Massimo (pictured), a shell-encrusted grotto, ten tiers, numerous parterres, obelisks and statues.

LEFT BELOW:
Restaurant, Cannobio, Lake Maggiore, Piemonte
In Piemonte cuisine, meats are often eaten raw, perhaps topped with a drizzle of olive oil. When cooked, meats are braised in regional wines such as Barolo, Arneis and Nebbiolo. A local vegetable is the *cardo gobbo di Nizza Monferrato*, a cardoon or artichoke thistle.

RIGHT:
Cannero Riviera, Lake Maggiore, Piemonte
The town of Cannero stands on an alluvial plain created by the River Cannero. This fertile soil, combined with the sheltered and sunny position, has encouraged the town's luxuriant camellias, azaleas and rhododendrons, as well as the many groves of lemons, limes, oranges and olives.

FAR LEFT:
Vernazza,
Cinque Terre, Liguria
Heading north, Vernazza is
the fourth of the five villages
of the Cinque Terre. It offers
the only natural harbour on
this steep and rocky coast.
The castle on the headland,
known as the Doria, was built
in the 15th century to protect
the fishing village from pirate
raids. At the same time, a
fortifying wall was built.

LEFT:
Riomaggiore,
Cinque Terre, Liguria
The most southerly of the
Cinque Terre and the most
easily reached by road,
Riomaggiore is also the most
visited of these picture-perfect
villages. A paved footpath,
called the Via dell'Amore
('Path of Lovers'), connects
the village with Manarola, the
next village to the north.
The path owes its name to
the fact that it offered an
easier route for young lovers
of the two villages, who had
previously been divided by
the vertiginous cliffs.

Boccadasse, Genoa, Liguria
To the east of central Genoa, the fishing village of Boccadasse has been absorbed by the city but still retains its old-fashioned charm. The village's name may come from the Genoese for 'donkey's mouth' (*bócca d'âze*), referring to the shape of its bay.

OPPOSITE:

Chiesa del Gesù, Piazza Matteotti, Genoa

On the central Piazza Matteotti is the Jesuit church of the Gesù, dating from the late 16th century. Inside is an intricate and slightly bewildering mass of gilt stucco and carved marble, as well as two paintings by the great 17th-century Flemish artist Peter Paul Rubens. Surrounding the church are the typical green-shuttered 19th-century houses of Genoa.

BELOW:

Antico Ponte Romano, Nervi, Liguria

A short bus ride east of Genoa is Nervi, once a fishing village and today a small resort. The village was already a port and staging post in Roman times, when the bridge over the River Nervi was built. Nervi is surrounded by citrus groves, while the seafront promenade is considered to have one of the loveliest views along this stretch of coast.

LEFT:

Savona, Liguria
The port city of Savona
was badly bombed during
World War II and was rebuilt
with utility rather than
beauty in mind. However, its
surroundings and its small
medieval centre are still
worth a visit. In the Ligurian
Apennines behind the port
is the Adelasia Nature
Reserve, protecting woods of
beech, chestnut, oaks, alder
and spruce.

RIGHT:

San Remo, Liguria
The resort of San Remo
had its heyday in the years
before World War II, when a
large community of Russian
aristocrats (and the composer
Tchaikovsky) made the place
their home. San Remo still
boasts one of Europe's
most famous casinos, glitzy
grand hotels and an elegant
seafront promenade.

101

Northeast Italy: Lakes and Mountains

Capital of the Veneto region, Venice was one of the world's first great financial centres. By the end of the 13th century, Venice's traders and bankers had made it the wealthiest city in Europe. During the Renaissance, the city's elite commissioned colourful works from the artists of the Venetian school, from Giorgione and Bellini to Titian, Tintoretto, Veronese and Bassano.

Travelling inland from Venice's island-studded lagoon, to the northwest is Vicenza, where 16th-century architect Andrea Palladio left the world 23 buildings of supreme beauty and harmony. A little further west is Verona, which does not disappoint the many tourists who flock to see the balcony made famous by Shakespeare's Juliet. For many travellers, Verona is the gateway to the Italian Lakes. These waterscapes delighted the Romantic poets Byron and Shelley – and everyone else of a romantic and less romantic disposition. Italy's largest lake is Garda, where gardens and lemon groves spill down the slopes to waterside *palazzi*. Further to the west, Lakes Como and Maggiore are included in the Northwest Italy chapter. To the north of Garda, no less beautiful but far less comforting, are the jaggedly eroded rock walls of the Dolomites.

OPPOSITE:
Lake Braies, Trentino-Alto Adige
In the autonomous, mostly German-speaking, region of South Tyrol, Lago di Braies is also known as the Pragser Wildsee. According to local legend, the green, pine-wrapped lake is the gateway to an underground kingdom.

Abandoned building, Dolomites

The Dolomites form part of the Eastern Alps. These ranges are generally lower than the Western Alps, with the highest peak in the Dolomites being Marmolada at 3343m (10,968ft). Around 250 million years ago, the range started out life as a coral reef beneath the Tethys Ocean. Tectonic forces, ice ages, wind and rain have made the scenery we see today.

Lake Misurina, Veneto

At 1754m (5755ft), the low-humidity microclimate and pure, unpolluted air of Lake Misurina are supposed to be beneficial for people with asthma and other respiratory disorders. In 1956, the speed skating events of the Winter Olympics were held on the lake – the last time they were ever held on natural ice.

LEFT:

Santa Maddalena, Val di Funes, Trentino-Alto Adige
The rugged Odle massif rears its head above the Val di Funes and the pretty Alpine church of Santa Maddalena. The Sass Rigais is the highest of these jagged peaks, at 3025m (9925ft).

RIGHT:

Lake Resia, Trentino-Alto Adige
Lake Resia was created in 1950 with the building of a hydroelectric dam. The flooding of the valley submerged all but the steeple of a 14th-century church, as well as 163 homes. When the lake freezes in winter, it is possible to walk to the steeple.

Colfosco, Val di Badia, Trentino-Alto Adige
Many of the inhabitants of the Val di Badia are Ladin speakers. Ladin is a Romance language spoken only in Dolomitic Italy; it has some similarities to Swiss Romansh and to Friulian, which is itself spoken only in the Friuli region of northeastern Italy.

San Candido, Val Pusteria, Trentino-Alto Adige
Close to the border with Austria, the small market town of San Candido, known as Innichen in German, hosts the annual international Snow Sculpture Festival in January. In summer, the valley is popular with hikers and climbers heading for the 'Three Peaks' of Cima Grande, Cima Occidentale and Cima Piccola.

Madonna di Campiglio, Trentino-Alto Adige
The upmarket ski resort of Campiglio also draws summertime hikers for the Dolomiti di Brenta. These rough peaks are known for their glaciers and the *vie ferrate* (literally 'iron ways'), a series of ladders knocked into the rock faces. Unsurprisingly, these white-knuckle climbs are not to be attempted during thunderstorms.

LEFT:

Cathedral, Trieste, Friuli-Venezia Giulia
Like many things in Trieste, the Cathedral of St Justus is a fusion of styles and influences. Its exterior is largely Romanesque, with the addition of a Gothic rose window. During the 20th century, Trieste was passed between Habsburg, Italian and German rule. Today, Trieste belongs to Italy, while its hinterland is Slovenian. The city is one of Italy's most multicultural.

OPPOSITE:

Interior of the cathedral, Trieste
The chapel of St Maria Assunta is decorated with a 12th- to 13th-century Byzantine mosaic showing St Justus, Christ and St Servulus. It was laid by master craftsmen from the Veneto.

Piazza Unità d'Italia, Trieste
With an area of over 12,000sq m (130,000sq ft), this central piazza is often said to be Europe's largest square next to the sea. It is lined with municipal buildings, including the late 19th-century town hall (pictured). On its tower, two automatons, named Mikeze and Jakeze, strike the hours.

NEAR RIGHT:
Le Sartine, Trieste
'The Seamstresses' chat as they sew an Italian flag and watch Trieste's waterfront traffic go by. The bronze statue has become a much-loved symbol of the city. It was installed in 2004 to commemorate the return of Trieste to Italy in 1954.

FAR RIGHT:
Marina, Trieste
In the 18th and 19th centuries, Trieste was the Habsburg Empire's most important seaport, making it one of the wealthiest cities in Europe and eclipsing even neighbouring Venice. Today, the city is once again an important trade hub, forming a link between Western and Eastern Europe.

BOTTOM RIGHT:
Miramare Castle, near Trieste
The castle was built in 1856–60 for Archduke Ferdinand Maximilian of the House of Habsburg. According to legend, anyone who spends the night in the castle will meet a bad end. As Emperor of Mexico, Ferdinand Maximilian was executed by firing squad in 1867. His nephew, Archduke Franz Ferdinand, stayed here on the way to his infamous assassination in 1914.

Venice, Veneto

Venice is sited in the shallow Venetian lagoon on 118 islands, linked by 400 bridges. Only 55,000 people live in the city itself, yet it receives up to 30 million tourists per year. This can give the city the feel of a theme park – yet it is the most magical theme park it is possible to imagine.

Grand Canal, Venice

The view from the Ponte dell'Accademia, one of four bridges across the Grand Canal, displays the elegant *palazzi* that line Venice's main waterway as it curves down to the Punta della Dogana at the tip of Dorsoduro. Dorsoduro ('hard back', due to its more stable soil) is one of the city's six *sestieri*, or districts.

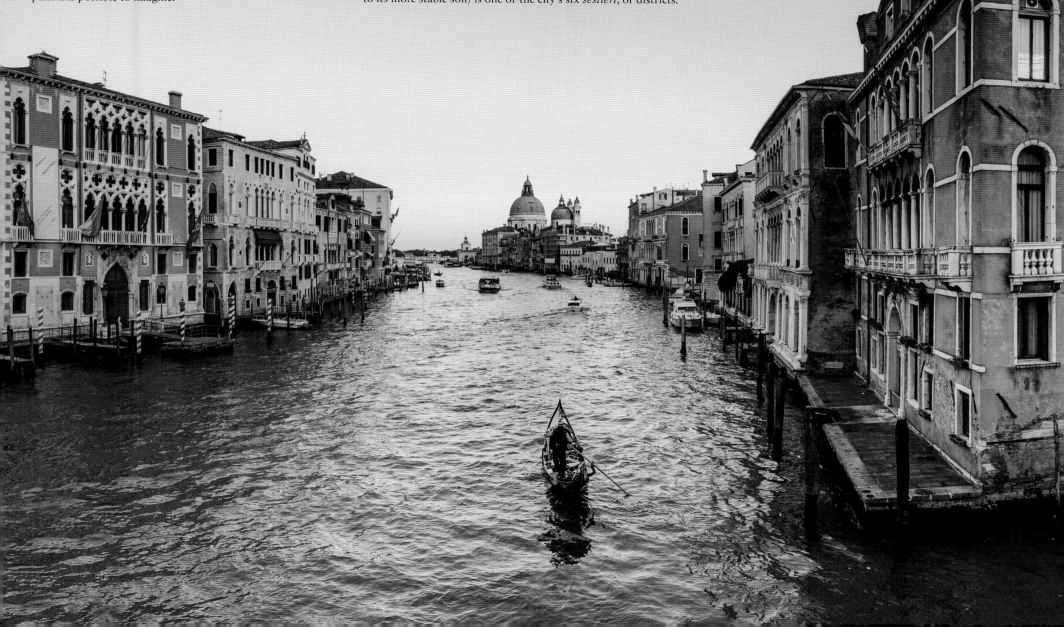

Punta della Dogana, Venice
On the narrow finger of land where the Grand Canal and the Giudecca Canal meet is the Dogana di Mare (customs house). To the right are the domes of the 17th-century Santa Maria della Salute (Our Lady of Health). This Baroque church was built to give thanks after a particularly devastating outbreak of the plague.

OPPOSITE:

Piazzetta di San Marco, Venice

The piazzetta connects the Piazza San Marco to the waterway of the lagoon. On one side is the Doge's Palace, built in Venetian Gothic style in the 14th and 15th centuries. This was the residence of the Doge, the Republic of Venice's elected ruler. In front of it stands a granite column crowned with a Lion of St Mark, erected in around 1268.

ABOVE:

Ponte di Rialto, Venice

Designed by the aptly named Antonio da Ponte and completed in 1591, this single-span bridge was the only way to cross the Grand Canal by foot until 1854, when the Ponte dell'Accademia was built. Two ramps, lined with shops, lead up to a central portico. When first constructed, the engineering of the bridge was so daring that naysayers predicted it would collapse.

121

Gondola, Venice

Gondolas are flat-bottomed rowing boats, perfectly designed for negotiating the shallow and often narrow waterways of the city. A gondolier sculls rather than punts with the oar, which is not fixed to the hull. In 2010, the first female gondolier gained her licence from the guild of gondoliers, after passing the tough training, apprenticeship and exam.

Carnival, Venice

Every year, the carnival takes place in the two weeks leading up to Shrove Tuesday. The tradition is said to have begun to celebrate a victory over the nearby city of Aquileia in 1162. The carnival is famous for its masks, which in medieval times were constructed only by members of the mask-makers' guild.

Rialto fish market, Venice

Near the Rialto Bridge in the San Polo district is the early-morning fish market. Probably around 950 years old, this market is one of the few places in Venice where you are likely to hear only Italian spoken. In medieval times, everything from slaves to furs and weapons was also on sale here.

Molo, Venice

The broad stone quay of the Molo is backed by (from left to right), the Zecca (the Mint), the Libreria Sansoviniana, the red-brick Campanile, the Doge's Palace and, linking the palace to the prisons over the Rio di Palazzo, the Ponte dei Sospiri (Bridge of Sighs). By popular consent (although probably not in reality), the enclosed bridge got its name from the sighs of the prisoners being escorted from the interrogation rooms in the Doge's Palace to their cells.

125

OPPOSITE:

St Mark's Basilica, Venice
According to legend, St Mark was told by an angel that his body would rest in Venice. To fulfil the prophecy, Venetian merchants stole the saint's relics from Alexandria in 828 and brought them here. The present basilica was completed in 1094. The majority of the Byzantine mosaics, most with a glittering background of gold glass tesserae, were completed by the 1270s.

RIGHT:

St Mark's Basilica, Venice
The basilica was intended as an advertisement for Venice's wealth and power. Built in the city's own opulent, cosmopolitan image, the domes are Byzantine, the plan is a Greek cross, and the whole concoction shimmers with mosaics and polychrome marble from Palestine, Egypt and Syria. The four horses on the balcony above the portal are replicas of the originals, which were probably Roman works from the 2nd century.

LEFT:

Murano, Venetian lagoon

Murano is reached by *vaporetto* across the Venetian lagoon. The *frazione* (parish) is on seven islands, linked by bridges. In the background of this photograph is the tower of an old glassblowing factory.

LEFT BELOW:

Mural, Murano

Murano's fame as a centre of glassblowing began in 1291 when the Venetian authorities, fearing a fire risk, ordered all foundries to Murano. The parish's glassmakers led the world in the craft for centuries, using multicoloured, crystal and enamelled glass to create everything from wine stoppers to chandeliers.

RIGHT:

Burano, Venetian lagoon

While Murano excelled in glassblowing, the ladies of nearby Burano became world-famous for their lacemaking. Today, very few ladies still practise the eye-achingly intricate skill, but some can be watched at work in the Scuola del Merletto and lace shops. The bright colours of Burano's houses are said to have enabled the settlement's fishermen to spot their homes from the sea.

OPPOSITE:

Palazzo del Capitaniato, Vicenza, Veneto

This *palazzo*, built in 1565–72, is one of the 23 buildings designed by Renaissance architect Andrea Palladio in Vicenza. The design of the loggia shows Palladio's debt to the ordered, harmonious architecture of ancient Rome. In common with other buildings that Palladio designed in the last years of his life, the façade is rich with stucco decoration.

RIGHT:

Teatro Olimpico, Vicenza

Designed by Palladio shortly before his death in 1580, this is the oldest indoor theatre in Europe. Seen here is the *scaenae frons*, the permanent architectural background of a Roman theatre stage. The backstage vista of a street seen through the arch, made from wood and plaster, was added by Vincenzo Scamozzi for the theatre's first performance.

LEFT:
Vicenza, Veneto
Soaring above most of the surrounding buildings are the green-roofed Basilica Palladiana and its slim 82-m (269-ft) clocktower. The clocktower pre-dates Palladio's 1546 design for the basilica, which essentially consisted of the supremely elegant propping up of an existing but unstable structure.

RIGHT:
Basilica di Monte Berico, Vicenza
Sited on top of a hill overlooking the city, this basilica was built in three months in 1428, after the Madonna appeared to a farm worker named Vincenza Pasini. She promised him that, if a church was built on the hill, the city would be free from plague at last.

RIGHT BELOW:
Villa Capra, near Vicenza
Palladio designed this graceful country villa for a retiring Vatican priest. The symmetrical, domed building, also known as 'La Rotonda', was inspired by Rome's Pantheon. Construction began in 1567, but neither Palladio nor the villa's owner lived to see its completion.

LEFT:
Giardino Giusti, Verona
These fine formal gardens were created by Count Agostino Giusti in the 1570s. The Renaissance design includes terraces, a maze and several parterres. The gardens were considered so exemplary that the Giusti family was allowed by the Austro-Hungarian emperor to change its name to Giusti del Giardino.

BELOW:
Amphitheatre, Verona
The amphitheatre was built in around 30 BC, when Verona was an important Roman city at the intersection of several trading roads. The amphitheatre is the third largest in Italy, after Rome's Colosseum and the amphitheatre in Capua, Campania. It had seating for 25,000 spectators in 44 tiers of marble seats.

OPPOSITE:
Ponte Pietra, Verona
The oldest bridge in Verona, the 'Stone Bridge' was completed in 100 BC. It provided citizens with a route from the city to the amphitheatre on the river's opposite bank. The arch on the far left is the only one that escaped destruction by retreating German troops during World War II. The other arches were rebuilt with original materials in 1957.

LEFT:

Madonna Verona, Verona
The Madonna Verona statue dates from the year 380, but was added to a fountain in the city's Piazza delle Erbe in 1368. Behind the fountain can be seen the 16th-century murals of the Casa Mazzanti.

OPPOSITE:

Piazza delle Erbe, Verona
The name of Verona's central piazza translates as 'Square of Herbs'; it has been a marketplace since the time of the Roman Empire. At the far end of the square, next to the Baroque Palazzo Maffei, stands the 14th-century Gardello belltower.

LEFT:

Limone, Lake Garda, Lombardy
Squashed between the mountains and Lake Garda, the pretty village of Limone was only reachable by road after the 1940s. Its name comes not from the area's many lemon groves but from being on the *limen* (boundary) between two communes.

LEFT BELOW:

Maderno, Lake Garda
On the western shore of the lake is the resort of Maderno. The majority of the mountains that tightly flank all but the southern portion of the lake belong to the Baldo Group. The lake is so large that it has its own microclimate, being milder and sunnier than the surrounding areas.

RIGHT:

Riva del Garda, Lake Garda
At the northern tip of the lake is the attractive resort of Riva del Garda. Strong winds make it a popular windsurfing and sailing destination. Ferries link the town with the resorts and picturesque islands of the lake.

OPPOSITE:

Malcesine, Lake Garda
A wedding party spills out onto a terrace in the village of Malcesine on the eastern shore. Behind the town is the ridge of Monte Baldo, reached by cable car or well-marked trails. The trip offers lovely views of the village, lake and retreating mountains.

BELOW:

Punta di San Vigilio, Lake Garda
The promontory of San Vigilio stretches into the lake at its widest point. On the tip, beside a small harbour, is a hotel, greenhouse, church and the remains of a Roman villa. This was a spot favoured by Winston Churchill.

RIGHT:

Rocca Scaligera, Sirmione, Lake Garda
This 13th-century castle was built by the Scaligera family of Verona. Its crenellated walls enclose a harbour for their fleet. The surrounding village of Sirmione, on the southern lake, is one of Italy's top spa resorts.

**Gardone Riviera,
Lake Garda**
This was Garda's most
fashionable Belle Epoque
resort, a fact still revealed by
its well-maintained botanical
garden, palatial villas and spa
hotels. The grandest hotel of
all is probably the 1884 Grand
Hotel, whose geometric tower
has become a landmark.

143

LEFT:

Piazza Santo Stefano, Bologna, Emilia-Romagna
The city of Bologna has some 38km (24 miles) of porticoes, or covered walkways. The first, wooden porticoes were built in medieval times and were so useful for protecting the residents from rain and sun that many more were built in stone.

OPPOSITE:

Due Torri, Bologna
In the Middle Ages, Bologna boasted 180 defensive towers. Today, only a handful remain, including the 97m (318ft) Torre degli Asinelli and the worryingly off-centre 48m (157ft) Torre Garisenda. Both were built in the 12th century by wealthy families.

Southern Italy: Il Mezzogiorno

Naples is the first city of the Italian South, which is known in Italy as *Il Mezzogiorno* (literally 'Midday', meaning 'south'). Naples is the capital of Campania and the birthplace both of pizza and the feuding Camorra crime families. A short drive from this edgy and decidedly real city is the ethereal Amalfi Coast. Here the jewel-like villages of Amalfi and Positano cling to the cliffsides above the Gulf of Salerno. In the shadow of nearby Mount Vesuvius are the ancient sites of Herculaneum and Pompeii, frozen in time by the eruption in 79 AD.

Succeeding rulers left their mark on the Puglia region, which covers the 'heel' of the Italian boot. Arabs from North Africa ruled briefly in the 9th century, leaving the city of Bari with a labyrinthine kasbah of an old town. Generations of feudal lords gave the Itria Valley its cone-shaped dry-stone *trulli*. Italy's 'instep' and 'toe' are formed by the regions of Basilicata and Calabria. Inland are the wild mountains of the Aspromonte and Pollino ranges, while Italy's strangest townscape can be found at Matera, where the *sassi* cave dwellings were dug into the rock itself.

OPPOSITE:
Amalfi Coast, Campania
The Sentiero degli Dei ('Path of the Gods') footpath links the hilltown of Agerola with Nocelle, passing through some of Europe's most bewitching scenery. The cliffs here are so steep that generations of farmers have maintained terraced gardens, carved into the slopes.

LEFT:

Via Chiaia, Naples, Campania

One of Naples' most high-end shopping streets is Via Chiaia, in the city centre. It was on this street, in Pizzeria Brandi, that the Margherita pizza is rumoured to have been invented in 1889 to honour the Queen of Italy, Margherita di Savoia. Sadly, the story may be apocryphal, as the tomato, basil and mozzarella pizza was enjoyed long before 1889.

BELOW LEFT:

Bar Nilo, Naples

Outside the Bar Nilo, not far from Naples Cathedral, is an altar to Argentine football legend Diego Maradona. While playing with Napoli between 1984 and 1991, wearing the number 10 jersey, he helped the team to two league titles, one Italian Cup, one UEFA Cup and one Italian Supercup. In his honour, Napoli's number 10 shirt was later retired.

BELOW:

Caffè Gambrinus, Naples

This legendary coffeehouse was opened in 1860. A haunt of Naples' politicians and artists and even, on one occasion, Pope Francis, the Gambrinus is the place to try traditional Neapolitan pastries. Top of the list must be *sfogliatella* (called 'lobster tails' in English) and *colomba* ('Easter dove' bread), which is offered in chocolate and pistachio flavours.

Piazza del Plebiscito, Naples
The city's main square is named after the plebiscite (or referendum) of 1860 that took Naples into the unified Kingdom of Italy. The colonnaded church of San Francesco di Paolo, which is heavily reminiscent of Rome's Pantheon, occupies the square's western side.

LEFT:

Fish market, Naples
Every morning, the city's fish market spills out from Porta Nolana onto the surrounding streets. Vendors offer enormous live octopuses, which still squirm as they are chopped, as well as squid, clams, mussels, oysters, seabass, swordfish, anchovies and sardines.

OPPOSITE:

Backstreet, Naples
As Italian cities go, Naples attracts relatively few tourists, in part due to its not-undeserved reputation for street crime. Yet visitors will be rewarded by views of its unglossed streets where washing is perpetually drying, its crumbling churches crammed with overlooked masterpieces, and the constant sounds of buzzing scooters and the hard-to-grasp Neapolitan dialect.

Castel dell'Ovo, Naples
Jutting into the harbour on the small Megaride peninsula, 'Egg Castle' takes its name from the legend that it was built on top of a magical egg placed by the Roman poet Virgil. The story goes that, if the egg had broken during construction, Naples would have been destroyed. In reality, the castle was built on top of earlier fortifications by Holy Roman Emperor Frederick II in the 13th century, although it was much rebuilt in the 17th century.

Palazzo Reale di Capodimonte, Naples

Built from 1738 as the residence of Bourbon King Charles VII of Naples and Sicily, the palace now holds one of Italy's best collections of art, based on the remains of Charles's own formidable art collection but much added to over the years. Highlights include works by Botticelli, Mantegna, Raphael, Caravaggio and Titian.

Castel Nuovo, Naples

Brooding over central Naples is the immense bulk of the 'New Castle'. It was built in 1279 for King Charles I of Naples and Sicily, when his capital moved from Palermo to Naples. In 1470, the white marble triumphal arch was squeezed in between two defensive towers to commemorate the taking of the city by its first Aragonese ruler, Alfonso I, in 1442.

Naples and Mount Vesuvius
Overlooked by Mount Vesuvius, there was a settlement on the site of Naples as early as the 9th century BC. By 750 BC, the Greeks had staked a claim to the spot, naming their colony Neapolis (meaning 'New City'). After the Normans took the city in 1139, it was passed from one dynasty to the next, including the Angevins and the Aragonese.

FAR LEFT:

Crater of Mount Vesuvius, Campania

At the summit of Vesuvius is a cone partially circled by the rim of a summit caldera, caused by the collapse of a much taller structure. At present, Vesuvius is 1281m (4203ft) high. It is regarded as the world's most dangerous volcano because of its violent eruptions, coupled with the fact that 3 million people live in its vicinity. The last eruption was in 1944.

LEFT:

Herculaneum, Campania

At the foot of Mount Vesuvius, the wealthy Roman town of Herculaneum was buried in ash during the eruption of 79 AD. The town had been mostly evacuated, but there were undoubtedly considerable casualties, with most deaths a result of the intense heat of the pyroclastic flow. The ash preserved large sections of the town almost intact. Excavation of the site began in the 18th century.

LEFT:

House of Neptune and Amphitrite, Herculaneum
This house, named for its beautiful mosaic, is one of the best preserved in Herculaneum. The mosaic, which pictures the sea god and his wife, is on the wall of an 'indoor garden' room complete with a fountain. The work was executed with great style and skill, suggesting that the owner of the house was wealthy.

OPPOSITE:

House of Julia Felix, Pompeii, Campania
Just down the coast from Herculaneum, the busy Roman town and port of Pompeii was buried under volcanic ash and pumice in 79 AD. Deprived of air and moisture for 1500 years before their excavation, the town's homes and artefacts provide an incredible insight into Roman life. This large villa, with a courtyard garden, was owned by a woman called Julia Felix. She converted the property into rented apartments after it was damaged by an earthquake in 62 AD.

OPPOSITE:
Odeon, Pompeii

Next door to a larger, open-air theatre, which was used for drama, the roofed Odeon was for more intimate performances, such as music concerts and poetry readings. Built in 80 BC, the venue had seats for an audience of 1500 and a wooden roof to help with acoustics. Behind the stage is the remains of a long dressing room.

BELOW:
Villa of the Mysteries, Pompeii

This suburban villa is named for its frescos, which are believed to show a young woman being initiated into a religious school, often called mystery cults because of their secretive rites. This portion of the fresco shows the initiate's mother (on the left) approaching a seated priestess. In the corner of the room, the shawl-wearing initiate seems to be momentarily panicking.

House of Marcus Epidius, Pompeii

This large home had an imposing atrium, with 16 columns with Doric capitals around an impluvium (a basin to collect and drain away rainwater). We can guess at the houseowner's name from the number of times it appears in election propaganda on the façade, as well as on the walls of neighbouring houses.

LEFT:

Casts of victims, Pompeii

It is thought that many of Pompeii's residents had managed to evacuate to a safe distance before Vesuvius's deadly pyroclastic flow. However, it is estimated that around 2000 of the town's 20,000 inhabitants died while attempting to flee, probably from the intense heat. Their bodies were covered in ash, eventually leaving hollows that archaeologists subsequently filled with plaster. This appears to be the final resting place of a family.

BELOW:

Forum, Pompeii

As in all Roman towns, the Forum was the heart of Pompeii. It was a public square where markets and meetings were held, surrounded by temples, government offices and the basilica, where legal cases could be heard. To the left of this photo, the two-tiered limestone columns are remains of the forum's portico. Fluted Doric columns lined the ground level, while Ionic columns surrounded the first-floor covered walkway.

ABOVE:

Positano, Amalfi Coast, Campania
This bathing platform, cut into the rock over the Gulf of
Salerno, belongs to a chic hotel. Occupying the south side of
the Sorrentine Peninsula, 25km (15 miles) south of Naples, the
Amalfi Coast is widely regarded as Europe's most beautiful
stretch of coastline. It is a UNESCO World Heritage Site for its
dramatic cliffs and Mediterranean woodland.

OPPOSITE:

Crypt of Salerno Cathedral, Campania
The port of Salerno lies at the eastern end of the Amalfi Coast
and is a point of entry for many visitors. The cathedral's crypt
is believed to hold the body of St Matthew, brought here in the
10th century. It is a riot of polychrome marble, added in the
18th century. The ceiling frescos depicting the life of the saint
were painted by the prolific Mannerist Belisario Corenzio.

Amalfi Drive

The SS 163 Amalfitana is one of the world's most thrilling coastal drives, complete with dizzying drops, hairpin switchbacks and narrow viaducts to bridge the gaps where carving the roadway out of the cliff face became simply impossible. The route is famed not only for its views but for the distinct lack of caution shown by many of its drivers.

RIGHT:

Atrani, Amalfi Coast

Perched on the cusp of the sea, Atrani has a surface area of only 0.12 square kilometres (0.05 square miles). The belltower of the Rococo Church of St Mary Magdalene, with its distinctive brown tuff, was built in the 18th century.

Ceramics, Amalfi Coast

The Amalfi Coast has been a centre for ceramics production since the 15th century. The local mineral-rich clay is shaped, fired and hand-painted with riotously colourful, bold, simple designs. Many traditional ceramics feature the lemons that are grown throughout the peninsula and turned into the ubiquitous and highly alcoholic liqueur limoncello.

Vietri sul Mare, Amalfi Coast

At the eastern end of the Amalfi Coast is the town of Vietri, known for the landmark of its domed Church of St John the Baptist. The 17th-century dome is covered in majolica tiles, as would be expected in a town famous for its potteries. Founded by the Etruscans and expanded by the Romans, Vietri is the largest town on the Amalfi Coast.

LEFT:

Amalfi, Amalfi Coast
Today, Amalfi has a population of around 5000, but in Byzantine times it was a great naval power, with a population of 70,000. Amalfi was defeated by the Normans in 1073, then devastated by an earthquake in 1343, but there are still relics of its past importance, including the 11th-century cathedral.

OPPOSITE:

Positano, Amalfi Coast
Rising up a pyramid-shaped hill above a sandy bay is the chic resort of Positano. During the Middle Ages, Positano was a port of the Amalfi Republic, but it fell on harder times, with half of its inhabitants emigrating to the United States in the 19th century. In 1953, renowned author John Steinbeck helped to rejuvenate Positano's fortunes when he wrote a glowing article about the fishing village.

Bari, Puglia

Bari's old town, perched on a headland, is a maze of winding alleys, shadowy passageways and dead-end courtyards, designed to protect the inhabitants from wind and sun, as well as to confuse invaders. It has the same effect on tourists, who will lose their way no matter how good their map.

OPPOSITE:

San Nicola Pellegrino, Trani, Puglia
The soaring Romanesque cathedral of Trani was begun in 1099 to house the relics of St Nicholas the Pilgrim, who died in Trani in 1094. This Greek pilgrim became ill while passing through the town, winning over local people with his goodness and miracles. The cathedral gets its almost ethereal glow from the pale white-pink calcareous tuff from which it is constructed.

BELOW:

Castel del Monte, Puglia
The Hohenstaufen Holy Roman Emperor Frederick II had this castle built in the 1240s on lands he had inherited from his mother, the Norman Queen Constance of Sicily. The highly unusual octagonal castle, with an octagonal tower at each corner, can be seen on the Italian one cent euro coin. At the castle's centre is an eight-sided courtyard.

Aspromonte National Park, Calabria

The River Amendolea winds between the Aspromonte Mountains. Aspromonte means 'rough mountain'. The southern Aspromonte are one of the few places in the world where bergamot, a fruit used for its scented oil and as a flavouring in tea, is grown.

Pollino National Park, Calabria

Italy's largest national park encompasses the Pollino and Orsomarso massifs of the southern Apennines. Between the great cliffs of the Timpa Porace and Timpa di San Lorenzo is the narrow Raganella Gorge. This sparsely populated region is home to rare Apennine wolves, black woodpeckers and spectacled salamanders.

LEFT:

Sassi, Matera, Basilicata

Matera is known for its *sassi* (literally 'stones'), a neighbourhood of cave dwellings carved from rock. These dwelling places have their origins in a prehistoric settlement, perhaps dating back to 7000 BC, but were added to by generation after generation, creating whole terraces of troglodyte homes.

LEFT BELOW:

Trulli, Itria Valley, Puglia

These conical dry-stone houses are unique to this region of Puglia. The *trulli* may owe their existence to generations of feudal lords, who ordered the people working their land to build their homes without mortar so they could be dismantled whenever tax inspectors arrived. Despite the *trulli*'s temporary nature, their thick walls offer good insulation against heat and cold. Today, many surviving *trulli* have been turned into holiday lets.

RIGHT:

Matera, Basilicata

Matera is positioned on the edge of a ravine, where the *sassi* were carved out. In early modern times, wealthier cave-dwellers built ordinary homes on the plain above. In the 1950s, the remaining troglodytes were forcibly rehoused in the modern town. Today, some of the *sassi* are used for hotels and bars.

Italian Islands: Jewels in the Crown

I taly has 350 offshore islands in the Adriatic, Ionian, Tyrrhenian and Ligurian Seas. The largest of them, Sicily, boasts a scattering of archipelagos as part of its autonomous region. Among them are the Aeolian Islands, eight rocky volcanic territories named after Aeolus, god of the winds. Mainland Sicily has extraordinary treasures from all its colonizers, including the Greek theatre of Taormina and the Norman cloisters at Monreale.

Thickly forested and mountainous, Sardinia is Italy's second largest island. On the north coast, the pink granite bays of the Costa Smerelda are the most expensive real estate territory in Europe. Also drawing travellers to its pristine beaches is the third largest island, Elba, part of the Tuscan Archipelago. Napoleon was exiled here in 1814, along with his personal guard of 600 men. Unsurprisingly, he escaped in 1815.

The Bay of Naples cradles several pretty islands. Despite the crowds, Capri's dramatic cliffs, caves, rock arches and stacks make it as alluring today as it was for pleasure-seeking Roman emperors. Across the bay is Ischia, where thermal springs surround the dormant volcano. Closer to the mainland is the smaller island of Procida, with its brightly painted fishing villages.

OPPOSITE:
Capri, Bay of Naples
The rocky bays of Capri are a popular stopping place for touring yachts and day-trip boats from Sorrento and Naples. Drawn to the island for much the same reasons, Emperor Augustus built villas, aqueducts and temples here. His successor, Tiberius, retired to Capri in 27 AD, leaving the empire in the hands of his unscrupulous aides.

LEFT:

La Martorana, Palermo, Sicily

Founded by the Normans in 1143, this church exhibits the many influences that have come to bear on Sicily over the centuries. The belltower (pictured) shows the impact of Islamic architecture on its Romanesque design.

LEFT BELOW:

San Giovanni degli Eremiti, Palermo

This much reworked church has its origins in the 6th century. After the Islamic conquest of Sicily in the 9th century, the building was used as a mosque. Once the Normans had taken power, King Roger II gave the church to the Benedictines in around 1136. Completed in the 1190s, the tranquil cloisters have delicate paired columns.

RIGHT:

Palermo skyline

The dome of Palermo cathedral rises above surrounding rooftops. The cathedral was built by Palermo's Anglo-Norman bishop, Walter of the Mill, in 1185, on the site of a former Byzantine church that had been used as a mosque during the Emirate. The building has been much revamped since, with the dome constructed in the late 18th century by Italian architect Ferdinando Fuga, who is also known for his grandiose public buildings in Rome and Naples.

ANNO · DOMINI · M·CCCC · LXXVIII

SAN
CT
VS   P·ETRVS

SAN
CT
VS   PAVLVS

Cappella Palatina, Palazzo dei Normanni, Palermo

This chapel, housed in Palermo's Norman royal palace, is a perfect example of the Arab-Norman-Byzantine style of architecture that was prevalent after the Norman conquest of Sicily in 1061. The shimmering Byzantine gold-ground mosaics were laid by Greek masters, while the wooden ceiling was carved by Arab craftsmen.

Palazzo dei Normanni, Palermo

The oldest royal palace in Europe, the Palazzo dei Normanni today houses the Sicilian Regional Assembly. The Norman kings transformed the castle of the Emir of Palermo into a multifunctional complex with both administrative and residential areas. The Maqueda Courtyard (pictured) was created by the Spanish in the 17th century.

LEFT:

San Domenico, Palermo
The Baroque façade of San Domenico was completed in 1726. In 1853, the church became the pantheon of illustrious Sicilians: it is the burial place of murdered anti-Mafia judge Giovanni Falcone, poet Giovanni Meli, painter Pietro Novelli, composer Errico Petrella, and many more.

OPPOSITE:

Palermo Cathedral
The cathedral's long history has made it a hotchpotch of different styles, but its western façade was designed mostly in the 14th and 15th centuries. The portico was created by Renaissance sculptors Domenico and Antonello Gagini, while the towers at either end were built in the 12th century in Arab-Norman style, with later additions.

FAR LEFT:

Backstreet, Palermo
The scooter is the transport of choice for many Palermitans. Most Palermitans speak both Italian and the Palermitano dialect of the Sicilian language. Although similar to Italian, Sicilian shows the influences of Greek, Arabic, Norman French and Spanish, among other languages, on its grammar and vocabulary.

LEFT:

Cannoli Siciliani, Palermo
Cannoli (meaning 'little tubes') are specialities of Sicily, consisting of tubes of fried pastry dough wrapping a sweet filling made from ricotta and often flavoured with pistachio or chocolate. Palermitan cannoli are fist-sized, but in other regions the pastries may be no bigger than a finger.

BELOW:

Good Friday procession, Palermo
As on the Italian mainland, Good Friday is marked by lengthy processions. During the Emirate of Sicily, many Sicilians were Muslim, having converted out of true belief, pragmatism or compulsion. In 1240, those who had not converted to Christianity were expelled by the Normans.

OPPOSITE:

Cloisters, Monreale Cathedral, Sicily

The cathedral in the hilltown of Monreale, just west of Palermo, was commissioned by the Norman King William II. The arches of the cloister display the mingled Norman and Arab influences that made 12th-century Sicilian architecture unique. The 216 elegantly proportioned twin columns are slightly pointed in Arabic style, while the elaborately carved capitals are full of Romanesque invention: knights, monsters, flowers, birds and snakes.

RIGHT:

Monreale Cathedral

The vast mosaics inside the cathedral were completed by Greek and Byzantine craftsmen in just 10 years. On display are countless Bible stories, from the Creation to the Feeding of the Five Thousand; the martyrdom of several saints; and William II himself, founder of the cathedral. Shown here is the awe-inspiring yet compassionate figure of Christ in benediction, over the central apse.

Militello in Val di Catania, Sicily

With Mount Etna looming in the distance, Militello is on UNESCO's World Heritage List for its Baroque architecture. Among the town's great buildings is the 18th-century church of San Nicolò, constructed after the previous church on the site was destroyed by the 1693 earthquake. The Oriental-style dome was designed by local architect Francesco Battaglia.

Cinder cone, Mount Etna, Sicily

Around 100 cinder cones dot Mount Etna's flanks. These have built up from cinders and ash around lateral vents. Mount Etna is one of the world's most active volcanoes and is in almost constant activity. About a quarter of Sicily's population, around 1.25 million people, live on Etna's slopes. The volcano is a major source of income, both from tourism and its fertile soils.

**Greek theatre,
Taormina, Sicily**
Built by the Greeks in the 3rd
century BC, this dramatically
sited theatre was largely
rebuilt in brick by the Romans
in the 2nd century AD. The
Romans added the stage
buildings, which closed off the
view, and used the venue only
for gladiatorial contests.

LEFT:

Ragusa, Sicily

Almost entirely rebuilt after the earthquake of 1693, the hilltown of Ragusa is a UNESCO World Heritage Site for its extraordinary collection of Baroque buildings. In the foreground is the blue majolica-tiled dome of Santa Maria dell'Itria.

OPPOSITE:

Cefalù, Sicily

The popular resort of Cefalù boasts a magnificent cathedral, commissioned by the Norman King Roger II in 1131 in a typical Sicilian Romanesque style. The front façade is flanked by two sturdy Norman towers, each surmounted by a spire added in the 15th century.

Noto Cathedral, Sicily

Like the other towns of the beautiful Val di Noto, Noto had to be rebuilt after the devastating 1693 earthquake, which caused the deaths of around 60,000 people. The Sicilian Baroque cathedral was completed in 1776, with a harmonious façade of pale yellow limestone and twin belltowers.

Good Friday, Enna, Sicily

On Good Friday, thousands of members of the confraternities of Enna dress themselves in hoods and robes to process through the streets. The origins of the hoods may be in Spain. Sicily had Spanish rulers, the first of them Peter III of Aragon, for a full five centuries after the War of the Vespers in 1282.

Fundrò, Piazza Armerina, Sicily

The Baroque entrance portal of the 17th-century Fundrò church, also known as St Rocco, is carved from tufa. There are two pilasters on either side with feather reliefs. The portal is surmounted by an elaborate cornice. St Rocco was frequently invoked against the plague.

LEFT:

Sanctuary of the Three Saints, near San Fratello, Sicily

The town of San Fratello is named for the three brothers, Saints Alfio, Cirino and Filadelfio, who were martyred for their faith in around 251, during the persecutions of Emperor Decius. According to tradition, the brothers, along with their mother, were killed near Lentini, in southeast Sicily.

BELOW:

Poggioreale, Sicily

In 1968, the town of Poggioreale was all but destroyed in an earthquake that left 200 people dead and many thousands homeless. A new town for the inhabitants was built a few kilometres away, leaving the unstable ruins of the old town to the weeds and birds.

Corleone, Sicily
The central Italian town of Corleone is most famous for being
the birthplace of several Mafia bosses, including the ruthlessly
violent Salvatore 'Totò' Riina of the Corleonesi, and Tommy
Gagliano, once head of New York's Lucchese crime family.
The town is also the birthplace of the fictional Vito Corleone
in Mario Puzo's *The Godfather*.

Temple of Hera, Selinunte, Sicily
Before being sacked by Carthage in 409 BC, the ancient Greek city of Selinunte may have had 30,000 inhabitants, not including the slaves who served them. The best preserved of the city's temples is the Temple of Hera, built in the Doric style in the 6th century BC.

Stromboli, Aeolian Islands
Stromboli is the most volcanically active of the Aeolians: its cone, which has three active craters, sends up showers of sparks and glowing rock every twenty minutes or so. Despite this, the island has a year-round population of 500, with many more visitors in high season to its chic hotels and black sand beaches.

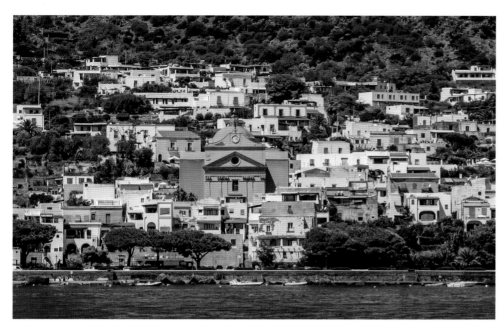

LEFT:

Santa Marina, Salina, Aeolian Islands
Occupying a central position among the Aeolian Islands, Salina has an area of only 27 square kilometres (10 square miles). The small port of Santa Marina is one of the island's two points of entry. Santa Marina is built on the site of a Greek settlement from the 4th century BC.

BELOW:

Salina, Aeolian Islands
Salina is composed of six volcanoes, the highest of them being Fossa delle Felci, which is 968m (3176ft) tall and visible to the left of this photo. The oldest of the volcanoes are hardly recognizable to anyone other than a volcanologist. The most recent eruption took place 13,000 years ago.

LEFT:

Lipari, Aeolian Islands
The largest of the Aeolian Islands, Lipari is the product of several volcanic eruptions, which created the island's peaks, obsidian streams and the pumice slopes that cover the northeast. Pale-coloured pumice from Lipari is shipped around the world. Lipari is still volcanically active, with the last recorded eruption about 1400 years ago and constant steaming from the many fumaroles.

RIGHT:

Panarea, Aeolian Islands
The little port of Panarea boasts most of the tiny island's 280 residents. Despite the island's small size and the fact there is only one paved road, Panarea is considered one of the chicest holiday spots in the Mediterranean. In ancient times, Panarea was larger than today: the volcano that created it sank partially into the sea.

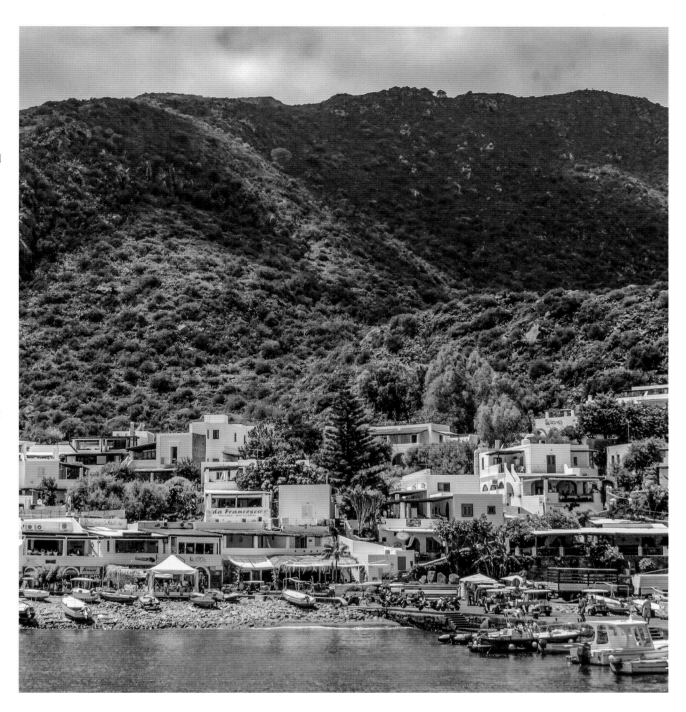

Faraglioni, Capri, Bay of Naples
The three Faraglioni, or sea stacks, of Capri are named, from left to right: Stella, still connected to the mainland; Mezzo, which has an arch; and Scopolo. Scopolo is the only home of the blue-tinted lizard. The town of Capri can be seen above the stacks, while the Sorrento Peninsula stretches into the distance.

ABOVE:

Capri, Bay of Naples

Despite the crowded summer months, Capri still has a
well-kept charm that has drawn tourists since the 19th century,
when the island's Blue Grotto was rediscovered. John Singer
Sargent, D.H. Lawrence, Vladimir Lenin, Graham Greene,
Gracie Fields and Mariah Carey have been among the long-
stayers on the island.

OPPOSITE:

Via Krupp, Capri

The switchbacking Via Krupp footpath leads down to the
Marina Piccola from near the botanical gardens. The path
was built in 1900–02 by German industrialist Friedrich Alfred
Krupp to connect his hotel and landholdings with his yacht.
Apparently, the path also led Krupp to a cave where lively
parties were held, a fact that eventually caused a great scandal.

LEFT:

La Piazzetta, Capri

La Piazzetta, properly known as Piazza Umberto I, is shaded by café awnings during the day and lit by twinkling fairy lights at night. The prices here are high, so locals head down a sidestreet for specialities such as *spaghetti alla pescatora*, *linguine ai frutti di mare* and a glass of Scala Fenicia.

LEFT BELOW:

Punta Carena, Capri

On the southwest tip of Capri, the lighthouse of Punta Carena has been in use since 1867. With a focal height of 73m (240ft), it is one of the tallest in Italy. Beyond the lighthouse, the Tyrrhenian Sea stretches to Sicily.

RIGHT:

Marina Grande, Capri

This crowded harbour is where ferries arrive on Capri, at the foot of Mount Solaro. The bay was also the point of arrival for the ancient Greeks. By Roman times, it was a busy fishing port. The houses of the port are painted in bright shades, including Pompeian red, one of the most intense colours traditionally used in this region.

LEFT:

Santa Margherita Nuova, Procida

On the headland of Punta dei Monaci is the church of Santa Margherita Nuova. The church and its neighbouring convent were built in the 16th century, but badly damaged by subsidence in the unusually cold winter of 1956. The church has been rebuilt, but the convent ruins remain unstable.

OPPOSITE:

Marina Corricella, Procida

Parts of the 1994 film *Il Postino* were shot in Corricella, the oldest fishing village on the island, where nets can still be found lying on the dock. By navigating the town's winding steps and terraces, visitors can reach the creamy-yellow Baroque church of Santa Maria delle Grazie, built in 1679.

LEFT:
Aragonese Castle, Ischia
The Aragonese Castle stands on a volcanic islet, connected to the larger island of Ischia by a stone bridge constructed in 1441. The castle has its origins in a structure built by Hiero I of Syracuse in 474 BC, but has since been rebuilt or expanded by many of Ischia's rulers, from the Romans to the Parthenopeans and Alphonso V of Aragon.

RIGHT:
Crypt, Aragonese Castle, Ischia
Under the shell of the cathedral (see below) of the Aragonese Castle is the crypt, built in the 11th to 12th centuries for the burial of local nobility. Some faded frescos dating from the same period can still be made out on its walls.

RIGHT BELOW:
Cathedral, Aragonese Castle
The Cathedral of the Assumption was shelled by the British in 1806 and has been in a state of ruin ever since. Before the bombardment, the 2000 inhabitants of the village surrounding the castle came here to worship – unless they chose one of the tiny islet's 12 other churches.

217

OPPOSITE:

Rio Marina, Elba

The port of Rio Marina was once busy with ships collecting iron ore from the nearby mines. Although the mines had closed by the early 1980s, sparkling, reddish iron ore can still be seen in the hills and picked up on the beach. The unusual hexagonal tower on the seafront, called the Appiani, was constructed in 1534 as a watchtower to foil pirate attacks.

BELOW:

Cheese market, Elba

Before the arrival of tourism, the people of Elba lived from fishing, farming and iron-ore mining. The tradition of cheese-making continues, with local cheeses including caprino (goat's milk), pecorino (ewe's milk) and ricotta. Other local produce includes red wine made with Aleatico grapes, as well as chestnuts, mushrooms and honey flavoured with eucalyptus or rosemary.

RIGHT:

Portoferraio, Elba

Portoferraio was originally named Cosmopoli ('Cosimo's Town') by the modest Cosimo de' Medici. The town remained part of the Grand Duchy of Tuscany until the late 18th century, when its strategic importance led to its being wrestled between France, Britain and Austria. Today, Portoferraio's stepped streets are often crowded with holidaymakers.

LEFT:

Portoferraio Lighthouse, Elba, Tyrrhenian Sea

The lighthouse was built in 1788 by Grand Duke Leopold II of Tuscany. The 25-m (82-ft) tower was a necessity to warn ships of the nearby shoal at Capo Bianco. Portoferraio is Elba's largest town, founded by an earlier Grand Duke of Tuscany, Cosimo I de' Medici, in 1548.

RIGHT:

Portoferraio, Elba

On the tip of Portoferraio's headland, beside the lighthouse, is Fort Stella, built by Cosimo de' Medici to defend his town from pirate attacks. To the left, the yellow house with green shutters, named Villa dei Mulini, was occupied by Napoleon during his exile here in 1814–15.

LEFT:

Costa Paradiso, Sardinia

The central section of the northern cost of Sardinia has been named Costa Paradiso for its secluded sandy beaches and dramatic granite coastline. The region is popular with walkers, windsurfers, kitesurfers and divers, who can explore wrecks and swim with groupers and stingrays among the red coral.

BELOW:

Bosa, Sardinia

In western Sardinia, Bosa is known for its multicoloured houses and narrow cobbled lanes, which lie just inland on the banks of the River Temo. The present town was founded in 1112, after the inhabitants of the nearby marina decided to move away from the sea to protect themselves from attack.

Costa Smerelda, Sardinia
The jagged, erosion-shaped coast of the Costa Smerelda ('Emerald Coast'), in Sardinia's northeastern corner, is popular with the jet-set crowd. The sandy beaches and pink granite cliffs are backed by *macchia* scrubland (known as maquis in France), perfumed by rosemary and thyme.

Picture Credits